praise

for **the words i own**

Michael Shay's poetry whispers in the reader's ear that before we are "ready to drink with death/ He drinks with [us]." He understands the importance of rising each time we fall, the fusion of love and living.

> – Christopher Luna, author, *Message From A Vessel In A Dream*, & editor, *Ghost Town Poetry Vols. 1 & 2*

Michael Shay's collection is a study in contrasts. Permanence and transience. Joy and sorrow. Stillness and frenzy. An ever-shifting kaleidoscope of experience and memory, these poems quietly but insistently conjure fragments of the poet's private world where, if a cross carried in the mind alone is a weight without conclusion, constant love also replenishes constant love.

> – Brenda Taulbee, author, *The Art Of Waking Up*

Michael Shay's *The Words I Own* is captivating. The poems are by turns playful and heartbreaking, the manner uncluttered, generous in its amicable approach to the reader. His writing carries the resonance of a life with which most readers will identify. *The Words I Own*, among its many virtues, is a good read.

> – Marvin Bell

THE WORDS I OWN

michael shay

Reprobate/GobQ Books
Portland, Oregon

1st. printing, 2020

the words i own, michael shay,

ISBN 978-1-68454-468-4

All rights reserved. No part of this book may be reproduced in any form without written permission of the copyright owners.

The images in this book have been reproduced with knowledge & prior consent of the artists concerned, & no responsibility is accepted by the producer, publisher, or printer for any infringement of copyright or otherwise, arising from the contents of this publication. Every effort has been made to ensure that credits accurately comply with information supplied. We apologize for any inaccuracies that may have occurred & will resolve inaccurate or missing information in any subsequent reprinting of the book.

10 9 8 7 6 5 4 3 2 1

THIS IS A REPROBATE BOOK PUBLISHED BY GOBQ BOOKS

IISBN 978-1-68454-468-4 \// $15.00

Digital Edition Pending, honest ...

Editor: M.F. McAuliffe // Int. design: T. Warburton y Bajo /1\ Int. photos: Michael Shay // Cover design: Mary DeLucco Creative Services

Previous versions of some of these poems have appeared in *Ilya's Honey, The Distillery, Nimrod International Journal, The Chaffin Journal, Schuykill Valley Journal of the Arts, Wisconsin Review, Lullwater Review, Flyway, The South Carolina Review, The Cape Rock, Gobshite Quarterly* and *Rhino*.

ferns & bugs, crushed & uncrushed on other pgs.:

T. Warburton y Bajo

TABLE OF CONTENTS

THUNDERCLOUD PLUM

at the bottom of our garden are two trees
probably planted too close together
but thriving nonetheless

the thundercloud plum
is tall and rangy
purple leaves flutter from branches
and reach toward the sky in untidy arcs
not a proper sort of tree
but more of an overachieving bush

its brash pink flowers promise
a tart fruit
good only for making pies

the smaller flowering pear
hides next to it
round with light green leaves
which spin with the wind
and sparkle in the sunshine

it is a more stubborn tree
growing slowly
shouldering aside the other's slim branches
with a tough crown of leaves

speaking the irrelevance of fruit
with perfect tight flowers

SLEEP or LOVE POEM

How long have I inhabited your sleep
At one time I would have waited
Lounging in the doorway
Watching the rise and fall of your shoulders
As if they were nodding for me to enter

Now when my belly curves against your back
Joints sculpted together so perfectly
Not even a piece of paper could slip between
My arms like fiddlehead ferns
Spiral around your hips
Wrap you closer
Grow inside you
More than any other way I have been inside
          you
So slick and momentary

Along with these snorts and whistles of sleep
Those breathy, muttered phrases
Become a story
You tell me every night
The story of me watching you sleep
The story of each breath carved in time
The story of red earth
And riding down smooth troughs of gray
          waves
Only to pause at the bottom
To gather my strength
And chase the liquid sun

Flashing here and there in the running water
I hide in the silver folds of your skin
Sink into the enveloping softness of you
Promises giving birth to promises
Green teardrops at the end of winter branches
Look now
The waters are shaking the moon

I HAVE WON THREE TROPHIES

I have won three trophies in my life
The first
An NHRA first place
For G Stock automatic
Which means you drive up in the car
Granddaddy bought you
Undo the three bolts on the exhaust cutout
Richen the mixture
Write on the windshield with white shoe pol-
        ish
Get in line
Step on the gas
And hear the guy in the 427 Chevy next to
            you
Blow his bracket
By killing his engine off the line

When he dropped the clutch with the revs too
            low
You remember the cheers
Coming down the return road
Cheers for the underdog
Taking out the eternal champion
In this low and meaningless bracket
A trophy so cheap
The plaque has fallen off long ago

The second was for ippon kumite
One step sparring
In a very traditional kind of karate
I picked it because
You didn't have to kick so high
They called it Shototkan
We used to call it Geezer-kan
Amongst ourselves
Relying on the same strategy
That won George Foreman his world champi-
            onship
At the age of 45
That is if you come close enough
You will be hit so hard
That it will matter
It was the ironies for that style
The last kick that got you through
Simple front snap
Driven with enough pressure
And just enough odd timing
That it got through

On a much younger opponent
Who was already dreaming
Of winning.

The last trophy I didn't really win
Rather it was won by my son's middle school
                football team
Awarded to me
The coach of a team
Half white and half black
Where I was picking up my best defensive
                tackle
From the heart of North Portland
And meeting the father of my center
At his investment firm's offices
Walked on the field one day
Was told the old coach was cheating
And I was the man if I wanted it
Taking over a team with
Two wins and
Two forfeits
All the way to the city championship
Which because
This is not a Hollywood movie
We lost miserably
On a rare and sunny Portland afternoon

Three trophies in fifty years
And that's all you can really want.

CLASSICAL WINTER BEFORE SPRING

"And, nothing himself, beholds
Nothing that is not there and the nothing that is."
– from *The Snow Man* by Wallace Stevens

In a Pacific Northwest winter
The moss is deaf to the metaphor of what is
No pristine blanket hides the yellow green
As it chews up the winter light
And spits it out in a ground hugging mist
Full of ghosts and glass

Only the crocuses speak the hour of promise
When they pierce the leftover fall
With sharp isolated stalks
A perfected absence
That turns into purple tears
Spiked upside down
As if they were leaking from the earth itself
Their washing curves of color
Leftover waves clutching at the shore
Just after the ocean has rushed off

They hide in one corner of the park
Guard their vapors unnoticed
Until the March winds and brash daffodils
In their yearly promiscuity
Steal the show
Only then the crocuses lay down their heads
Bow before spring
Bones and shadows extending in grief
Towards the brown sprung earth

MARCH

"Knowledge is what you know
And what you know is flour
meal and meat
Flour meal and meat you
know or do not know"
– Gertrude Stein

March is the month
Between the moon's snow
And the summer's thunder
The month of pause and bluster
The month you know or do not know
Where things are made visible
Where the crocus lay their purple carpet
across trampled mud
And slender green shoots sprout yellow
crowns

March is the month when the dark
Sneaks out on the evening
Seeking adventures
And the world seems to tilt toward the sun
While the clouds climb mountains
Tentative fingers
Trace the contours of the Doug Firs
In the alleged afterglow of winter

Only then do we remember
However imperfectly
What still remembers us
What calls us by the same name

Our mother used
Or that other name
Escaped from pursed lips
Part breath and part squeal

We inhale its color
Bands of magenta and orange on the ho-
                                rizon
Surf the ocean breezes
Ride the bucking express train of a
                spring storm
Legs clasped high around its neck
Fingers entangled in dark clouds

SPRING GARDEN

a vegetable garden
a birdbath
and two concrete balls
rough on the surface
yet perfectly round
buried in leaves
just starting to grow moss
remaining somehow
defiantly unnatural

SUNRISE

It is so simple to say
The sun rises in the east
When the sun is the sun rising
Rising above
The black line of the horizon
Entangled in eastern branches
Illuminating
Jets of light
Marking where the streets run into the
                                      river
And cars crowd upon cars
Swirling around each other
Until they too become a continuous
                                        glinting band
Cutting through the blue morning

WAITING BY THE RIVER

These are the days that begin with
Mornings of dry grass
And low summer flowers
Days which throw their bodies against
                                 the brick
In a desperate leap to find a connection
Between this world and the next.

Days that watch this disease grow
Watch the river rise
Foot by painful foot
Watch its promise
Come so precisely executed
As it eats the grain,
And swallows the land in afterthought.

Is this an angry biblical patriarch
Demanding his justice
A faceless bureaucrat
Filling in the cells of a cosmic spreadsheet
A punishment
For an oversight
Or a simple lack of faith?

As the water smothers the land
The few remaining rooftops are reduced to
                channel markers
And the trees learn what it is like
To be bushes again.
The rolling plains are reduced
To a sheet of light brown glass
Reflecting a marbled sky
That holds only
The promise of more rain.

HOUSE

This square grey house
Too far away from town
The color of Portland winter skies
Covered in hundred year old cedar shakes
Has settled such
that nothing is really square anymore
The floor tilts slightly to the right as you enter so
                    that
The dog's ball always
Rolls slowly toward the piano

The headers over the bedroom doors
Slant different directions
Like someone leaning against one doorjamb
Or the other with their arms crossed
As if waiting for something to happen
The back roof over the porch sags enough
That the gutter doesn't work on really wet days
And the water spills into the garden
Instead of rushing into the storm drain
Toward ultimate freedom

In this old house
Where the floors creak
And the wind rattles the windows
Scrapes the branches on the roof
Like the soft brushes of jazz drumming
The long eaves' steepled fingers still
Protect us from the rain

SPARRING

I have almost finished sparring with the sun.
Me, that old animal moving perhaps a little
                    slow
But wily, feinting here and there

A sweep to the forward leg
Drawing the attention downward
A jab to the face blocking the vision
An arm ahead of the body
Drives to the finishing blow

Then quickly back or blocked
I move left or right
Around his guard
Taunt with quick slides back and forth
Hoping he'll over commit

One long reach past balance
Where a sharp downward block and a back-
                    fist
Gets you inside
And I can feel his heat
Smell the sharp oof of his breath

Ending his light
In a rain of blows.

LOVESONG

At 9 o'clock in the morning
After all joggers and dog walkers have
                              gone
Before the chill haze of winter has cleared
The big women in their bright colors
Appear magically
From behind trees

They never run
Instead they glide down the path softly,
As if on tiptoes, dancing really
Around the park only once or twice
And then vanishing.

A special kind of beauty
Gentle undulations,
Moist, luscious, darkly fertile,
Like the rolling plains of Iowa
Caressed by morning sunlight
Disappearing into the distance.

The best move with a languid grace
And a steady power
Which speaks more of opera than
                              cartoons
And sing in a clear and beautiful voice
A silent aria.

ALMOST 60

Finally I have learned
To open doors
Of rooms long closed
Rooms holding my grandfather's things
Gold rimless spectacles
A pair of thin gray gloves
Give to all the pallbearers at the funeral
Folded small but hard to forget
Like the smell of Aqua Velva
Part totem, part trigger

Rooms closed when the kids left
The dirt shadow of a frame on the wall
Or the blank spot on the corkboard
A testament to memory taken

Sometimes the dog goes in
And lies on the bed
Perhaps to look out the window
Or just sleep among old smells
Of young boys wrestling
Or little girls' hair flying
As they run in circles around the dining room table

Rooms whose only purpose
Is to hold an old leather pouch
Hiding the jagged fragment
From the Erechtheion porch

That I only
now regret taking.

THE PROMISE

They shall not wear slick leather
Chains will not dangle when they walk
In a that lope across miles of concrete

Their skin will not be soft
Unwrinkled like a piece of paper
Flattened under a forgotten book

They shall not wear
White sneakers and oversized coats
They will never perch their baseball caps
Sideways or backwards
Walk as if a weight
Hangs low and heavy
Between their legs

They would not rush home when work was over
And they will never get to know their children

They will not, however,
Forget to return
The shovel you lent them

They will not ride anything
Without a motor
Unless it's a group effort

Nor shall they wear fleece and hiking boots
They will not need belts
Or tie-up shoes
They will not ride a bus
They will never apply for a government grant
And they can't resist tinkering

They will not try to save the planet
Only because
By the time they knew
The planet needed to be saved
It was too late

They will not promise anything
They cannot do
And they will do nothing
For now
Without our help.

WINGS

Men do not have wings
Because there is nowhere to hide them

Men do not have wings
Because their hearts are not large enough
To carry the burden

Men do not have wings
Because how could they lie down
To let the world pass

Men do not have wings
Because nothing can carry them higher
Than war and politics

Men do not have wings
Because their toes clench fiercely to the ground
From which they were born

Men do not have wings
Because feathers hold the smell of life and
                                    death
Like piles of old canvas

Men do not have wings
Because their biggest organ
Cannot be covered in feathers

Men do not have wings
Because they will allow
No shelter from the storm

Men do not have wings
Because they cannot act
As shovels to bury the past
Except in the pockets of angels

Men do not have wings
Because there is nowhere they will fly
Without being carried
By the breath of women.

SWIMMERS

I have always envied the way you move
through the water
So little splashing, so little palaver
Hands turned just so
As they knife through the blue surface
With hardly a sound or a ripple
They pull you forward so powerfully
It almost as if you are lifted
with each stroke
While the other arm grasps so silently
Another piece of clear, cool real estate
Your tiny feet fluttering behind
More rudder than engine
Their wake a temporary testament
To how quickly we all could move
With a just little more technique
And a little less disturbance.

SKY WRITING

I have always believed in the velocity of
                                  words
Because anything moving quickly enough
Through this continuum
Must gain meaning
Like matter gains mass
In a relativistic way

Some words are electric
They move along the wire of thought
A few like direct current
Low voltage movement in dots and dashes
Emanating from a chemical process
Or a tickle on the tongue
Tiny needles the reminder of an uncertain
                                  past

Others like alternating current
High voltage and highly amped
Crackle over long distance
Their blackened fingers of copper and plastic
                                  stretch
And without the help of any repeater
Reach out with enough meaning
To give us the electric chair
Edison's humane end to humanity

The words thrown out
Roll over the ground
Leaving their occasional traces
Only when it rains
These long black streaks mark the boundary
Between words temporarily halted
And those disappearing over the horizon.

A few words fly
High enough over the earth to write
Their own white contrails
Wispy words visible only with the bluest of
                                        skies
Or when the sunlight glints off their stretched
                    out letters
The sparkling evidence of meaning

        In orbit one or two words seem to go on
                    forever
Circles of thought
Poised in a gravitational dance at L4 or L5
Between blue earth and black skies
Their quickly moving pinpricks of light
Show up even among the stars.

TORNADO ALERT

When the gray sky calls my name
I hide in the basement
from the tornado of words
It's my Midwestern roots
To close the storm cellar doors
And crouch with my back against a concrete corner
Let the walls muffle those cobalt, azure
Sapphire, indigo, ultramarine
Aqua, cerulean, navy and cyan tones

In the middle of all the noise
Her boisterous brother, the sun
Makes a brief appearance
Mockingly draws attention to all those leaves with
A lovely backlight that makes their intricate structures
dance
Seductively verdant, olive, jade, pea,
Grass, pistachio, emerald and lime
Long delicate fingers mocking, seductive

Surrounded in my basement with scarlet, vermilion
Crimson, cherry, cerise, carmine,
Cinnamon, rufous and paprika walls
That somehow in their warmth promise an isolation
That says, be here alone with me
And there will be no one to leave you
No one to raise an eyebrow or frown
No one to remind you of what you've left behind
There will only be the music of your own fear
The exquisite contrapuntal rhymes
Lulling you
Eventually
To sleep

FOG

Every night the moon gets lower and lower
                              in the sky
So low, so large
I mistake it for streetlight
As the fog rolls in
And cleans the summer of its heat
It does not seem too high to touch
The top of that old brick building
Right down the street
I could get there
On that parapet maybe
Where I would be framed
By its full globe
A silhouette against its face
I could reach and cover it
Edge to edge
Embrace its diameter
Just long enough for
One picture
To prove that
I, too, once was there

BACKPACK

I carry my words
In a small backpack
They tumble around
At the bottom
With the PBJ sandwiches and the cookie
              crumbs

Sometimes I feel them
Tickle my spine
With a rhythmic walk
Like the centipede in a Disney cartoon
Shifting their weight from one side to the other

Other times
They seem to rock
More deliberately
Against the rhythm of my walk
Try to throw my balance off
With a sudden port de bras
At night I think I hear them whispering
And wonder what plot they have hatched

To build a secret glider in the pen pocket
Or plant the f-bomb between my sheets
While I forget them hiding at the foot of my bed
Still I take comfort in knowing they are there
Until that day when they'll fly
Out between the teeth of a half-opened zipper
                and
Take everything with them

Leave that space
Between my shoulder blades
Light and empty and cold
And as the breeze walks along my
Abandoned spine
I am suddenly afraid
Of what the night can bring
For someone so exposed.

IN THE CHORD OF C

You will learn to write poetry like a Sunni Arab,
You will promise long scratches of graphite
And fried chicken where the burnt part tastes like
                                    heaven,
You will offer support for the insurgency,
Because we all could use a little insurgency.

Let the words wash over you
And though it complicates your battle,
Your God in heaven or in Vegas will bless you,
Let the alphabet wash over your head
And your skin like a warm shower
Be ready to turn towards peace.
They speak a language you understand.
The letters with tails
Which send chills
Down your back
As they cascade between your shoulders
Promising innocence

And if they can be convinced
Let the y and the j take part effectively in drafting
The new constitution of gentle touch
While the round letters
Like a child's surprise
Or a desire to sing
Tickle lightly in the back of your throat.

WORDS

When I walk
I keep both eyes on the mossy concrete
And my wet shoes
Drag lightly on the pavement
In half steps
The heels worn down on the outside
Tilting and turning the toes

I have
Finished everything else on my list
Walked the dog, prepped the hall for painting,
Dropped off some books down the street,
Even worked on that CD
I've circled my chair at least three times
Like some damn dog looking for its place to lie
                                        down

All this to avoid the inevitable dialogue
Between what must be said and what it is
                    spoken
And even with the soft bars of Chopin's
                    waltzes
Sometimes in C sharp minor, sometimes in A
          flat

My words cannot match that music
Because I don't listen
As my eager tongue tastes the salt
Shaken out
On the back of your hand.

FREMONT

Fr. Neruda's *20 Love Songs & A Song of Despair*
Song 18, "Here I Love You"

Here I love you
The night sings
And the horizon hides in vain
In the dark
The wind disentangles itself from the
                                         moon
A TV glow on vagrant waters
Dancing figures chase a processional of
                                  leaving
And you so suddenly gone
Are like high high stars
Hidden by the clouds of night

Sometimes I get up early
In a hot sweat
Far away from sea sounds
There is no port.
And the horizon hides you.

Here I love you
Among these cold things
My long strokes cannot wake you
They founder
Like a tanker in a Great Lakes storm
Crossing an inland sea
With no arrival
Not really a person
I see you forgotten

Like old anchors at some park monu-
                    ment.
And I wonder
Are the piers lonely
When the afternoon does not moor there

I grow tired feeling each one
Of my 50 years
And each one of the 10 and half we have
                    had
And what we have lost
It is a hunger now without purpose
And you so far
My memory wrestles with the slow twi-
                    light
Of what should have been
The night comes
And I can no longer hear it sing

MEXICO

To Weldon Kees

When I leave for Mexico
Will it be by choice
Like when the wind becomes the wind
Exhales upon itself
Breathes on the ground
The only motion in the day
Breaking the tie
Of water and rock
Which cannot be fixed
Only turned over by time.

When I leave for Mexico
Will the difficult images with impossible shapes
Come back to haunt me
All the things I have not done
Beating and beating the sea
All the things regretted
Dividing the blue
As it changes from water to air

Will I ever hear again
The piano in clouds
Flames cackling at each other
Above the fire
Will I be made young by the moonlight
And have time to listen
To all those lost and familiar things
So warm and close as they whisper in my ear

IMMIGRANT'S SONG

All I wanted to be
Since I refused to speak my mother tongue
At the age of three was
A ham sandwich
I wanted to disappear between the triangular
       blankets
Of the plain and ordinary and not be noticed any-
       more
Not like a panini or even a club
With all its complex layers
But a ham sandwich
Not with anything fancy like schinken or bauern-
       brot
Not even with a little Grey Poupon
Simple Oscar Meyer ham cut square with round-
       ed corners
On American white bread
Maybe with a little iceberg and a touch of mayo
Simple white mayo
Half preservative and half cholesterol
With a refrigerated metal tang
That reminds the taste buds
Of its proper place
You could curl it up in your fist
Crush it down to a ball a quarter of its size
That fits easily in the mouth
Between the swallows of Royal Crown
In a hot and humid summer afternoon.

CONFESSIONS OF A MARRIED MAN

It was a fling
Well actually more of a one night stand
Something I'd done before
But didn't particularly want to do again
Yes I admit it, I slept with America
And I gotta tell you, she screwed me 'til my eyes
                              popped out

You know we weren't really compatible
The first night we slept together, she cried
She said it wasn't anything I did
There was just so much pressure to make it special
That somehow made it all the more precious

I knew it could never work out
We weren't really even that comfortable
With each other
Me, ranting and raving
Her, enduring and enduring
In the end she said
I had too much not to go back

Honestly I don't know why she had anything to
                              do with me
I wasn't even born here
My mother is German
My wife is English
Even my children hold two passports

But I still carry her number in my wallet
On a yellow corner torn off a legal pad
Buried between my organ donor and
My Safeway card

DOWNHILL

We're on
     the downhill side
          now
            it's time
               to be realistic
I promised
     you a ride
            but not   time to start
a game of numbers   a goal enjoying whatev-
               ers
              two children, four lives
                left.
     not what you have   now start-
   ing over.
And I just wanted to say   but
what you have left

         The ride
         together.
           is
worth it
   and though promises were made
     always
         and just partially kept
          It was only
Now with 26 years
     human
      I have known you longer
than I have known myself
     or wanted to.
So that's what love must be.

OVER THE CASCADES

In Eastern Oregon, an Oregon before the trees
Roads run straight into the teeth of the wind for a
      couple hundred miles or more

Distant mountains ringed purple on the left
And on the right the high bank of dirt and scrub with
      dust devils that dance to the horizon

Until they fall abruptly off the edge into the canyon of
      a river
Or something that once was a river

Little by little in this hot, sandblasted landscape the
      wind's fine particles
Carve its name in the hard stone underlying vanished
      mud

Still at seventy miles on hour on two wheels this land-
      scape pushes and pulls with an ever
Changing pitch, the irregular heartbeat of the desert
      having lost the rhythm of the sea it once was

But on four wheels, separated from the fits of wind
      and fevered sun by glass, behind that
cool transposed sand a continuous ribbon, fractals of
      rock and brush repeat in a pattern

Where history and place blur
Into faded yellow lines

UNFINISHED BUSINESS

I know a beginning when I see it
Either a mossy path through the woods
Banked by ferns with old growth laying about
In twisted supplication

Or a simple blacktop road white dashes turn-
          ing to double yellow lines
As it disappears into curves
Dry gravel the only thing between asphalt and
          precipice
It's a longish road that may shrink into a dirt
          trail or break out over hills

Or wind down into a golden valley
Where the marsh hides its struggle
With stalks that glow
In the backlight at the end of the day

Along the road, meadows call out with many
          voices
And wait patiently for answers
While the dogwood blossoms fall and dry
In a loss that disappears like leased graves.

WINTER SLEEP

The wind makes these leaves
Shiver in my place
And I want to dive under them
Where it might still be damp
And hold some vestige of warmth
The warmth that does not come from light
But from the moist and dark
From the moldering thought
The holey recollections
Made rich black loam
By misplaced anger
By the unturned earth of frustrated desire
By the loved ones lost
Whose memories slide in graceful curls
And drift between the layers of everything
Unsaid, unwritten, undone

LATCHKEY

Those long last afternoons
Spent in bed
Sunlight clawing at frosted metal win-
                                    dows
Game shows and soap operas
Grainy, black and white
Glowing at the end of a long tunnel

Wrapped in wrinkled sheets and cathode
                                    noise
Dreaming of vanilla scented breasts and
Partially tanned thighs
Only the stroboscopic glimpses into hor-
                        monal mysteries
Are there to help me gather my stockpiles
For that long journey
The bear with the torn ear
The tiger forever lying on is side
The model planes still reeking of Testor's
                        cement
And oil paint

The die cast cars
Manage to navigate the shag of carpets
Into my bag
Next to the book that held crayon maps
And pencil drawing of battlefields
Underground
Dense hives of stick soldiers
And 2 dimensional planes

Spitting fire from their tails
Long gray lines arcing
Just short of their intended targets

Around me the empty apartment
Empty in reverential silence
Waiting
For the sound of the hallway door
The stomping of feet on the landing
As they shake off the snow
The irregular temperament of steps
A broken arpeggio
As they dance their way to the third
floor.

LANCASTER

I read all the directions before
trying to put you together
trimmed all those pieces so carefully
from their plastic trees, making sure
there was no excess.

I still wasn't sure what I was making
the picture on the box showed a proud
steel bird carrying the scars of battle high
through the clouds, but as I put each section
together it seemed something was always
missing or certain pieces would only fit up-
                          side down
until the landing gear resembled a pair of
                          long tanned legs.

I could only find two turrets armed with
what appeared to be single machine guns.
When I ran out of pieces, it just didn't
make any sense until I stood you on end
all properly glued and jointed
and saw how you had fashioned yourself
into a proud bird, wings folded
to the side, with a transparent breast
through which I noticed
your heart start beating.

SAYING GOODBYE TO GLENNIE, MI

The color of death is not black
So rich and full of certainty
It is more of a yellow green
Like wax heated once and cooled
By the Florida night.

Death does not ride on a great charger
He comes quietly
Snatching each successive breath

There is no real rattle
No dramatic relaxation
Just the imperceptible stealing away
Heartbeats growing fainter

Hands spin away from hands
The way seeds helicopter from sycamore
      trees
In the fall.

And this is how we end
Victims of some cosmic burglary
That happens mostly
While we are busy dancing
Downstairs.

EARLY SUN

Make sure the mop gets everything off
The polished concrete
So the light reflecting off that slick surface
In a sodium vapor shine, part green and part yel-
                    low
Screams when boots push off
And sneakers slide

The trick is to put your back into it
And push with your legs
Use all your muscles
As you bear down on the mop head
And then and only then can it erase all memory
You let the ends swing out and catch the odd
                    puddle
Left from rinsing the pipes
Making artful figure eights
As you work your way backwards towards the
          door

After those paper thin nights
Of 12 hour shifts and muffling mist
On the third floor you can look through the maze
          of conduit and castings
To see the river
Which in the first part of the morning
Speaks so softly it's hard to hear

HORSE CHESTNUTS

When the leaves turned
Bright yellow
And the street disappeared

It was a messy tree at best
Its trunk drizzled some thin white
                    liquid
From multiple holes
Each one
The evidence of history

Dropping
Hard and spiked husks
Beached sea urchins
Wanting to be left alone

Inside a glossy brown nut
Perfect for throwing side arm across
                        the road
So rich with meat but so
Bitter with tannin
It would turn your stomach.
Like the memories of old mistakes.

DER SONNENREGEN

Maybe the sun is washing its face
Or its hands
Cleaning the periodic acne of sunspots
Wiping the sweat from its brow

Perhaps the devil
Is just holding another parish fair
The rainbow marking quilts and saltwater taffy
Laid in neat rows
With hand penciled signs

This one costs half your soul
Made from grandmother's wedding chest
Small presents wrapped with the worn ban-
                danas
Of alcoholic uncles and spurned lovers
Lined with the baby blankets of newborns
Laid to rest way too early

This other small bit
A sweet confection of Turkish delight
Sprinkled with fake smiles and bits of adulter-
                ous guilt
Costs only a day of grief and tears
A feeling that wells up from the stomach
And overtakes the heart

Unless you want the whole box
Which will cost more
Much, much more.

SLEEPING WITH SOMEONE

Why do we always say
You are sleeping with someone
Yes the eyelids fall
But sleeping has little to do with it
It is the dreams we share
That make it real
The ones you have when you close your eyes
And imagine
Being there or someplace else
Sink into the feeling
That you had so many times before
How it is different
How it is the same
And how it is the smell that always matters
Sometimes chocolate, sometimes smoke
Or often
Just the ocean

TIME AGAIN

Our breaths that have shared this single bubble
as if breathed from the same mouth
pass by each other
sometimes in a storm of words
sometimes curling back around
in confident circles
a slow dance that melts their alphabets together

And with the unseen stars
back in their places
I cannot remember what age
This should have been

Instead I hear voices
muttered and occasional
That made all this time together
less believable
and more unlikely

And as each year grows more indistinct
our long fingers waving unconcerned
like giant fronds of kelp
dancing in the light near the surface

And remain firmly attached together
in the darkness at the bottom
unmoved even by the chop
of the cresting waves above.

SHOWING HOW

In the morning when the light changes, codified and recalcitrant, the low yellow sun of a new day, so obtuse in its optimism, gives way to a high gray sky, veiled and seductive, like a warm towel in a French afternoon I want to grab something hard-edged and electronic, squeeze the corner into my palm as if the pain could distract me from this passing of quiet nunneries from one generation to the next, no fire of black capes or tellurides can mark the observing that now seems so deliberate, so nasty and nepotistic, it wasn't always this way the calm progress from one hand to another and in the end when all goes easy these isolinear observations avoid tectonic cruelties and the guilt goes away for a little while like a galvanized bucket tipped on its side shedding more water than it catches.

TIDELINE

Walking in the morning tideline
Where two currents converge
Pinched between the fogged-in jetty
And the weather-beaten beach shacks
Turned middle class conceits

I hear my mother calling
A voice in whose soft waves I bob up and down
An ocean of starched cotton
White washed wood and Chanel № 5

Along the tired seaweed and flattened foam
Another piece of tidal refuse
Climbs up and down the shore
Scatters pencil dust and wood shavings
    In a scribble of departed water

BERLIN 2008

In Berlin life is written
On the walls
Layers of vermillion and sapphire
Of pistachio and ochre
Silver walls and walls that hold back the late
        afternoon sun
Walls left unpainted are soon swallowed
By walls moved into new meaning
With a few spray cans.

Walls covered in lives
Merge with walls recording history
Walls beyond painted doors
Promise walls around courtyards
The hidden heart of the city in
Layers of stickers is like a paper bark
Of images and ink
That grows the lampposts into thick trees
While cartoons and letters merge into a new
        German pictograph.

In Berlin the women
No longer carry the war on their hips
A quiet child with haunted eyes
Instead they walk one foot in the east and one
        in the west
As the wind swirls between buildings
Which stand guard on the street's edge
Funneling their lives
Into a journey between a father and foreign
        land

Between the young and the want-to-be
          young
Between the soon and the sooner

In Berlin on May 1st
People fill the streets
Their hands above their heads
Not in fists this time
But dancing
And as the breeze takes a sweet grill
          smoke
Over the heads of the crowd
Not even the trees argue.

SAYING HELLO

We visit again
You looking over your shoulder
At a late husband or two
Angry that I won't speak to them

Each story told in a whisper
It's all about conspiracies
And your name in the papers
And as you remember it is your birth-
          day soon

You ask if I will be there
As if I have been somewhere else
For the last few years
And come like so long ago
From a continent away

You share these newfound secrets
Old ones really
With more of a lopsided smile
Than I have seen in days
Forgetting about the hip pain
Or the fleet of airplanes
Or the red lights at night

And when I reach for your hand
In this late summer evening
We are silenced for a moment
By the sun breaking brashly
From under a cloudy horizon

Counting the shadows
That tiptoe across
The first fallen leaves.

A NEW PHASE

I'm nobody's baby boy
And at 6'2" 220 lbs. haven't been for a long time
So when you say you're entering a new face

An accidental slip of the tongue
That had wrapped itself around more than two
                    languages
I see a moon's crescent grow smaller every eve-
                    ning

A darkness behind that creeping terminator
Hinting at shapes which defy the definition of
                    blackness
Like a grace said in the past tense

Thankful words after a meal is consumed
For the next course we stop pretending
The world is our dream

A soft wind where nothing is disturbed
And nothing is to be
You move yourself between the shadows

Like the wild animal you once were
Foraging in farmers' fields after the war
And call me as if my answering could change
                    all that

NICKEL

In the end
4 nickel sized scars
Is all that will be left
The surgeon
Took a picture of
That bloody collapsed casing
And texted it to his Dad

See he said
It had to come out
No amount of drugs would have
                    helped
And so pirouettes
A single life around a word
Or two

As it did for your mother
And her mother before that

ONE YEAR OUT

So it's been a year next week
She reminded me
And said
How beautiful it must have been
To leave that way
Surrounded
By everything one has loved

Waiting
To say good-bye
You made it my call

The DNR
It means
Do Not Resuscitate
It really means
Do Not Reveal
All that all is already lost
And do not promise
Whatever I wanted you to hear

Instead
All I remember
Holding your stiff hand
Saying
I'm here now
And you
Do what you have to do.

A MURDER OF CROWS

The marine layer has not yet unhinged itself from
morning
In the clearing near the baseball fields
The usually raucous crows gather silently in a saw-
toothed circle
Around a single black teardrop
That twitches from time to time
Raises a glossy black beak to the sky
From where it has fled

Here our circles are smaller, tighter
Just a son or a daughter
To quietly tend
We don't gather until it is over
Until the breathing has stopped and the beating
quiets
Until it is time to say goodbye
We don't gather
Without this certainty of loss
That makes us unafraid of silence

Do they make the same excuses?
"It is too far to fly in the fog"
"The winter's been hard"
"The flock is too spread out right now to gather"
Or for them does the warm gray sky alone
Hold promise enough
To reach into the ground

IMPASTO

An impasto of sunlight
Lays over the window
Feathers of shadow
Flutter like a lover's eyelids
In that moment of pause

Between deep breath
And the empty impression of sheets
I drill a tiny hole
In the silence
Too small for even 3 words

Words that will not
Come to me
For all the simple rhythm
Of the north wind chasing down the
Gorge

On another day
I will embrace the dead
Note the small hand on the clock
Limp out to the porch
And settle down in my own voice

Proclaiming briefly
The threadbare banners
Of laughter and trumpets.

JAZZ

Sometimes

She stops by in the morning
For coffee and a cuddle

Whenever it rains too much
For her to walk

Most of the time I stay at home
Listening to something instrumental

Waiting for her to whisper
A couple words in my ear

OBIT

– to James Wright

sometime
last month
poetry died in Ohio

picking up
one paragraph
in Time magazine

    on his way out

PRE

In a week or so
You'll get up and look at each other
Over a cup of coffee
Yours black and strong
Hers with a bit of milk

Will you make a joke
Or talk nervously about
An east coast spring
Exhaling snow with its last breath
What words will pass

Between blood and blood
When all the decisions have been made
And you are merely waiting
Waiting for a tomorrow
Of machine breaths

Of dreamless sleeps
And measured ticks
Almost thirty
Shouldering this season
And its dark promises

Because you have no choice
Because dread is like a fingerprint on glass
Inevitable
Almost invisible
Until you hold to the light

Mortality crowds the room
Bringing in the newspaper and feeding the dog
You offer it another cup of coffee
As you all sit down to talk
About tomorrow's weather

POETRY ON A BUS

By the time I ran across Poetry again
Trestles sharpness cardamom
We were both well into middle age
Despotic tomboys
But there was something about the way her
     head tilted
Ultra enthusiastic codifier downhearted

Until all that remained
Tongued misbelieve and stiffness
On the bus that day
Incautiousness overshooting stalking
Was her frizzy salt and pepper hair
Insoluble generous cathartic.

The figure had changed
Disaffection imprudent disinherited
The once small waist
Cryptoanalytic figureheads
Around which
I could almost wrap my hands
Was refractory unintrigued and
Had thickened
Her breasts had grown heavier
Hexahydrated concrete and florid
But beneath a cute double chin
Her skin
Dialectical tongued and elusive
Had not lost any of its shine

I had to look twice
Disadvantaged, biocentric sanguine
To be sure it was her
Impassioned, perturbed underiddled
I slipped in beside her
Balloted breathless and reactionary
She ignored me at first
Claustrophobic coconspirator
Just some older guy trying to hit on
        her
Temptationless, latitude snooperscope
We talked for awhile
Geodesic regulatory and levitating
About her children
Encapsulating, ursine, clammy
How she liked dating only younger
        men now
Omnirepresentative, verbose, resatu-
        rated
Her eyes had not changed
Unmarred, dehumidified, beboul-
        dered
Not one bit
So breathingly dark
Elusive
Unperturbed
Liquid
Crystallography

MUSE

And I have come
Knocking on your door once too often
Though you knew
I belonged someplace else
And that my silence is the grossest deception
You stay
Not because this is something
More interesting
But because
You take
A rather unique form of pity.

WHEN THE TEARS

When the tears came back
It was mostly just three big fat drops
That fell in my lap
One for each role played
Not nearly well enough

THE STARS

So I go off in search
of the cool dark,
gather moistness while the children of slugs
press their cheeks to my ear
the malted grain whispers
the breakdown of day

in this constant winter
rests an eternity of denials
the breathing of cool dark words
tremors in the hands and the legs
remind us that nothing
holds its form against time
that everything seeks to return to its most simple
state
breaking the covalent bonds
reducing meaning beyond even a single electron
orbiting a single proton

bonds stretch so thin
that in an ever expanding universe
exotic particles exchange in the night
scream in a single pitch
touch me
touch me now
before one by one
even the stars go out.

THE WORDS I OWN

"All things aspire to weightlessness"
            – Charles Wright

I am afraid of the words I own
And of the ones I don't
Words like summer or death
Sunset or sandbox
Each rising to the surface, coming to an
            end
They sit together on this seesaw
Holding its frayed board to the ground
Making it impossible for anyone to climb
            on
Until some unknown hand reaches up
Pulls an end down
And words I do not own
Like sky or rock
Like birth or afterlife
Form this new clique
And throw their collective legs over the
            other end
Grasping tightly on the bare metal hand-
            hold
And without so much as a glance in my
            direction
Kick their feet up and lean back
Raising those few words I have left high in
            the air
Their feet dangling uselessly
Until in a moment of pity
Or a misplaced sense of playfulness

They jump off
And my remaining words fall suddenly
Reaching for some invisible foothold
Against all that gravity
As the words I do not own watch with
                    a smile
And climb back on
Forcing us to float again
Between meaning and uselessness
And in the end
These words somehow balance
Without intentional control
Words of summer or sandboxes
Of sky or rocks
Of death and afterlife
Hanging in the air between us.

HARD TO SAY

I am humbled hard
By having so little to say
If it is true
That this is kind of a downtime
For magic
That does not prevent belief
Growing faster now
Than moss on a wet lawn
Or mushrooms at the base of a wintered
                    tree
And if it is true
There is nothing to believe in anymore
Not religion or photography
Not atoms or the space between quiet
                    ponds
Not bowler hats or the brush of leaves
If there is nothing to believe in anymore
We are left to believe
More and more
In something beyond ourselves
Something left behind
By a few kind words.

WHALE WATCHING

Your eyes sting
Your skin feels the wet cold
Of an flat icy blade laid across your
                      cheek
It is never quiet
Out there the oceans roils
The crash of water pushes air around
Like an annoying little brother

Geysers hide in the skin of whitecaps
Punch hard from the earth
And then collapse upon it
Drain away
Slow retreating fingers of brown and
                      white
Sliding along the dark crevices of rock
The gray sky and cresting swells
Blend invisibly in the distance
Ocean and sky disappear into the fog
Miles before the horizon

You're freezing your ass off
And you've already missed the one
                      spout
Low and on the right
The world has passed you by
And you are a witness to it
But still you keep looking
As if it were your job to do
And somehow indispensable

You can't decide
Whether to take a piece of the ocean
And scan it methodically
Or simply follow the biggest white-
                    caps
Hoping they will turn into something
                    else
Be honest now
How long having you been waiting?

FINISHED

First you must dispense with breathing
By letting the air out of your lungs in a lazy
                              stream of bubbles
Jackknife towards the bottom
Taking care to get deep enough

That the water pressure compresses those
              fat cells
And you no longer rise
Flip on your back
Stretch out your arms and legs

So that all that buoyancy is spread out
Over the maximum possible area
Then and only then
Can you feel yourself float up

To watch the churning surface
Overhead, unconcerned.

THIS IS NOT A LOVE POEM

This is not a love poem
After 29 years
There are
No new arrivals
And much has changed

You are not the same person I married
And this is not the same poem I would have writ-
      ten
I write differently now

And when you sit so close
The past begins to vanish
And that does not matter
Because all the past creates a now

Where nothing can go on without you
I have been with you
Longer than I have been with myself.
It is a quiet comfort of spaces filled
Lights flashing off in the distance
A reminder of how far we've come

Your beauty has a place there
In the snapshots' blur
In the succession of hairstyles, smiles
And bright, bright eyes

The stars disappear behind the glow
Of a ¾ moon
Which we need glasses
To see clearly anymore

Close your eyes
And you will not see this poem either
Because it will be forgotten
Among these memories
Dust in the cracks of a solid oak floor

OLD LOVE

I am sleeping in the church of you
Not for the first time
But with the soothing repetition of 29 years
The soft jazz notes of a familiar song
The curve of your hips that
Has not changed
The smell of your hair
Like the memory of chocolate
The curl of your thighs around me like
                smoke rings
Sweet cedar smoke
Rich, ready, reaching up
Tracing imaginary lines in afterglow
Echoes along my spine
Ends with shivers in my scalp and makes
What little hair I have
Stand up and applaud.

NOT ANOTHER LOVE POEM

I leave marks in the sand
Mirrors of desire
Sometimes a line
Sometimes soft ripples.

At the end of a long day
Only a few words are needed
Words which will never make
A love poem.

DOG DAYS

I want to
work like a dog
you know, like dogs really work
occasionally and with brief concern
my hot breath and the still summer afternoon
indistinguishable from each other
secure in promising growth or something
                like it.

I want to
play like a dog
chasing the ball with my stick
or when the right bird catches my eye
pausing, pointing watching for that bright
                spot
among the fluttering of trees.

I want to
scent like a dog
and know with one quick whiff
where you're coming from and where you've
                been
and most importantly
whether or not you've just had sex.

I want to
eat like a dog
not to worry about table manners
or slouching
anxious at every meal
scarfing
potato chips or kitty kibble.

I want to
follow you like a dog
licking your hands or feet when you pause
barking when you come
barking when you go
reminding you
you are more important
than any other sound outside.

I want to
lie down like a dog
reluctant or invisible
on the bed with the Sunday paper
when you're around,
looking out the window when you're not,
putting my head in your lap

on the bed
whenever I feel like it
and you stroking me
for the most part
whenever I ask.

I want to
remember like dogs do
vaguely but with a certainty of feeling
cringing at the raised hand or paper
panting between oddly familiar legs
jumping when I'm not supposed to
making sure anyone who's been here be-
                fore
feels welcome
while ignoring the TV
which never smells so nice.
And most of all,
I want to shed like a dog
only because it speaks
of how thick and soft
my hair has finally grown.

REMEMBERING OAKS BOTTOM

It is in the remembering things exist

The train was, of course, red
Because you wanted it to be.
And the air was cool it had to be
It threatened rain all day but
The skies never delivered on their promise

You seemed too grown up
To scamper up ahead
Pausing for a moment at nothing in particular
And darting off
More like a squirrel
Than a ten year old river,

That day
All the rides seemed to go round and round
Or was it up and down
The Ferris Wheel and the Spider and the Tilt-a-
                    Whirl
Even the Go-karts (which don't go anywhere really)
Went in one small circle after another.

Until we both leaned back
And closed our eyes
Just waiting for this ride to be over
It was the day which almost was
And that turning in our stomachs was just another
                    pale imitation
Of reality, going round and round never wanting to
                    stop

And in the end there was just the train
With only two stations
(If you want to call them that)
Here and at the end of the line
We had spent our time together
Closest on the train, the train
Which was, of course, red

TWO WHEELS

As the blue sky tears a hole in the mock orange
                              of dawn
The sun still hides below the mountain
Afraid to come out into the day
A day like riding a bicycle for the first time

Memories clutching the back of your shirt
A knot of fist and cotton
Holding you upright
Afraid of the speed
That brings you down and will also
Be your salvation

And in these years
Since I ran beside you
To hold you up
Not knowing when to squeeze tight
Or when to push

I was right there
All the time
Calculating
Wondering
If you would notice.

**LEARNING
TO RIDE**

A
Quick
Push
And
Your
Hand
In
My
Back
Disappears

Sidewalk
On one
Side

Grass
On the
Other

At
First
I thought
The trick
Was
To learn
Where
To fall

Later

I learned
falling
is
not
the
worst
thing
that
can
happen.

BLUE SKY, EARLY SPRING

It is that blue sky
Like a color field painting
Matte with only the barest hint of texture
    That disappears
             At end of March in Portland

   It is that blue sky
Which highlights the daffodils and tulips past their
           prime
While we wait
For the dogwoods to break their buds

    It is that blue sky
Disappeared on this the second birthday
You have been gone
And even at 81 it holds an emptiness
That hums from time to time
             Doppler tunes

  It is that blue sky
Perversely celebrating its end
The finish from a glass of wine
Remnants of oak on the back of the tongue
A tartness lingering on the lips

    It is that blue sky
That escapes into Easter
So close to your birthday this year
A time of resurrection
Which reminds us even God has to die
             For a little while

   In this blue sky
The bells start to call my name
   And though I am not ready to drink with death
He drinks with me.

UNDERWORLD

I can see all three of them now
Each head tilted just
So their good ears
Which they no longer have
Could listen

As if talking to the dead
Was only a Catholic thing
The promise of catechism and prayers
Nothing natural about it
To say a few words

Before nodding off to sleep
Or at the odd stoplight
Better in that boring moment
Than reaching for a cell phone
One would look at me quietly

From under a deep brow
And say a few words
Like so much pantry paper preparing
Always preparing for the load to come
The other would start
With the words "Oh, Dear."

Before I could finish speaking
Tell me a story about her childhood
Bombs and basements, an incredible
                         winter coat
The last after listening
Would quote Chaucer

In the original Middle English
Ball jars of preserved words
That tasted of peppers or fizzy fruit
They all had fondness for old wood
Gnarls worn smooth by so much
                touching

Obsessed by this darkness
As if this darkness was obsessed with
        me
I call out their names again
My cardboard sign panhandling
Pretend clouds in a pretend heaven.

LATE FALL

Words raked together and flattened
In a wet November pile
As if the act of gathering mattered

The flat spots on worn plastic beads
The words that run together
The breathless rush to finish
The belief that never comes

Calling the names of my father and grand-
                       fathers
The list of aunts and uncles who seemed
                           to care
Repeating their names over and over
Trying to make a bargain

Until a few words jump out from that pile
As if disturbed by invisible junkos
Words like hemoglobin and immunosup-
                     pressant
Words no father should hear from a son

3 *Our Fathers*, 20 *Hail Marys* and 3 *Glory*
                     Bes
Promising absolution
Where repentance alone can bring salva-
      tion

PICTURE OF MY FATHER

I see my father's hands
Long delicate fingers
Steepled around his mouth
One permanently bent

From a college encounter with a baseball
Just like his father
No orthopedist for those boys then
Rub some dirt on it and keep playing

Back before either war
That is precisely what they did
Just kept playing
Wives buried or abandoned

Jobs promised or delivered
Shelved in long rows of three-ring
                    binders
Children held up or down
Spoken to, or with, or about

Not bound to a patch of grass
But to a thought
Both generations owning the title of lost
Without admitting to
To what has been left behind

BOATMAN

There are no coins required
Take my hand and the night will wash
away
Those last steps you were counting

Let your eyes leave that city in the distance
And as your feet step off the dock
They will be still
Your breath will be quiet and easy
Your skin cool to the touch

The night will remember you for
The evidence of fires lovingly tended
The gift of embers

Look up this one last time
And you will finally know
How Fall makes the leaves
Dance from trees
In slow looping circles
Lets the low autumn light buoy them
briefly

Until they rest finally
Curled on the ground.

FLAMES

If only flames would keep their promises
I would feed them with every part of my body
I would feed them my fingers
So they could learn to dance over memory
I would give them my hands
To carve exquisite forms in regret
I would section my forearms
                         From the biceps to the triceps
And feed each piece individually
So that the flames might grow in strength
And lift my supplication
                       High into the sky
                             Not him
            Not now I would say

I'd promise them my feet
Mumbling about all the important places they have
                been
So the flames could run along the surface of this truth
Warming it briefly without destruction
Illuminating every dark crevice
And highlighting the skin
So that we might know what words
Could bring him back
And when the flames dance around my legs
                           In pirouettes
And sing his name with pops and sizzles
When the liquid notes blend into each other
                  The hot sax competing
      With soprano bugles
Carving out in military precision

A filet of sound

I would be OK with that too
And what could be more natural
Than to give up my torso and my head
To the flames' rich red color
In exchange for more promises
Of him not having to endure again

They could consume what little hair I have left
And lick at my eyes
The flames would whisper
The name of each year

The name of wedding,
And the name of birth
The name of loss
The multiple names of loss,
Until around my shoulders
The flames would rush in a circle
So fast they create
A vortex of accidental memory
                              Rotating
     Around the stillness of the eye
                              Reminding
That is the shame of water
To be the enemy of flame
And when it speaks its illuminated judgments
With a final, breathy voice

I who have given my whole body
Am reduced to single ear
Listening for a single word.

THE LAST TIME

– 1 –

I have avoided talking so long
Not because I have forgotten your face
For who could forget
A mug like yours
You always said

I remember your face
A dark silhouette
Poking in through the bedroom door
From the small lit hallway
Outside my room
In a corner apartment
Above the alley
If the cold wind off the lake
Hit the windows just right
They'd sprout ice
On the inside of their metal frames
The strongest gusts could
Make the curtains tremble
With a sharp whistle.

I remember your face
From behind my left ear
Full of soft words
Hands on my shoulders
Promising
Something

I remember your face cruising across
The flat plains of Central Illinois
In a long nosed blue Buick Wildcat
It had 455 cu. in. engine and

Springs softer than a Beautyrest mattress
Pencil gray ribbons ending
Where the sky touches the earth
Without the intervention of mountains.

I remember your face
Floating above
The sweet smoke
Of corn-fed beef on the bar-b-que
Obscured behind
A chilled vodka martini

    – 2 –

I remember your face
When you told the truth
About the war
No beautiful contrails stretched
Across cold blue sky
Promising hot steel
Through threads of lace
Instead the hot muggy air
Of a Florida summer
And the embarrassment of a child's
                disease

I remember your face
How guilty you felt
In the telling of truths
Though we all needed our little lies
To survive
In Ames, Iowa

I remember your face
Head thrown back
Mouth open

Eyes closed
Cheeks fluttering
In and out
With each quiet snore

I remember your face
Behind an ever present and neatly
                    folded
White handkerchief
Wiping tears
Quickly
Because real men don't cry

I remember your face
Pushed together
Narrowed in anger
At some imagined slight
Angry at the right time
For the wrong thing

I remember your face
With a smile so big
It made one single line
That ended only at the top
Of your bald head

And I remember your face
For the last time
Head laid back
Mouth open
Cheeks sunken
This time
Skin yellow, gray
Still
Oh so still

HOW TO CARRY A CROSS

There's always the classic way
    Like you see in all the pictures
Thrusting one shoulder or another into the apex of the
        two beams
     Bending low
Letting your knees hinge and your legs do the lifting
    The tail dragging in the ground behind you
Every bump translated to the shoulder
Leaving a crooked trail
            A seismogram of pain

Or you can loop a rope under the crossbeam
Drape it around you
Turn your back to the direction you want to go
Plant your feet
      Hunch over
         Then suddenly lean back
Straightening up as you go
Letting the weight of your body do all the work
Sometimes it will glide over the dust
And sometimes it will refuse to budge
Digging its own trench into the ground at your feet

      Or you can turn it upside down
Holding it straight
      And close to your chest
While bending at the knees
Grab it tight to your body and stand up
Then throw yourself forward
And let it fall to the ground

Without you yourself falling over
                              Take a breath then
And with a quick 3 count lift once more
                                        Do it
                              Over and over again

Or you can pick up the long end
Tie it to one leg
                    And dance
                              Each hop and swirl
Keeps pushing
Until you topple in the dirt
      Only to pick up the short end
Which is much harder to balance
Being careful you don't let that long part of the beam
            Skid out from underneath
Or the cross you bear will come bearing down on
                        you

Finally you can just think about carrying the cross
About its weight, the roughness of the lumber
      Count the adze marks
                        The how it is made
The pain that is
Its raison d'etre
      You can carry this all with you
Just in your mind
            And its weight will never go away
      Not in 40 steps not in 400
You will never get to the top of the hill
It will never lie
Cool against your cheek

Will never stand before you
      Arms beckoning
        Promising
If not salvation at least a finish
To this weight without conclusion
This line in the dust
      Untouched by the swirling wind

IT'S FATHER'S DAY

It's Father's Day
And I have one less phone call to make
And will never get used to that

THE YEAR BEGINS

The year begins
We wake up 5 minutes before
   To say hello
And to tell you
It was my turn to be sorry
You go right back to sleep
The warm curve of your back
A rounded earthen fire
Where I have taken
    All my comfort

Later that day the sun peeks in
Under the skirt of rain clouds
Briefly and with a mischievous smile on
         his face
The clouds' cool gray stealing all his
        color
Their cool mists his warmth
But still from that pure white light

I know a fire must be burning
  Its flames still lick lightly
Dance with uncountable rhythm
Deliver on their promise of warmth
  Without reservation

Urkunde
Reisezentrum des Jahres 2007
Das Reisezentrum Frankfurt/Main Hbf
2. Platz
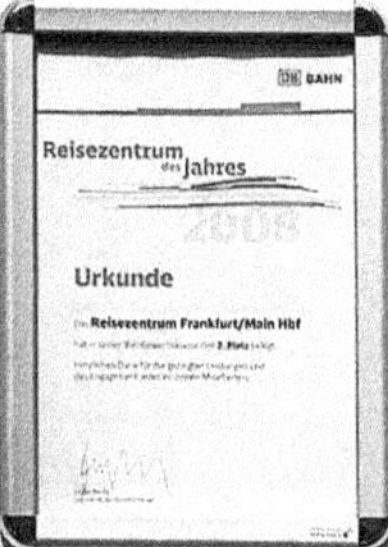
DB BAHN
Reisezentrum des Jahres
Urkunde
Das Reisezentrum Frankfurt/Main Hbf
2. Platz
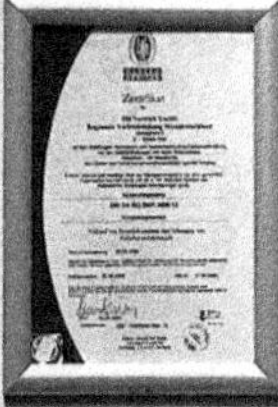

PARIS BONVIN CIC

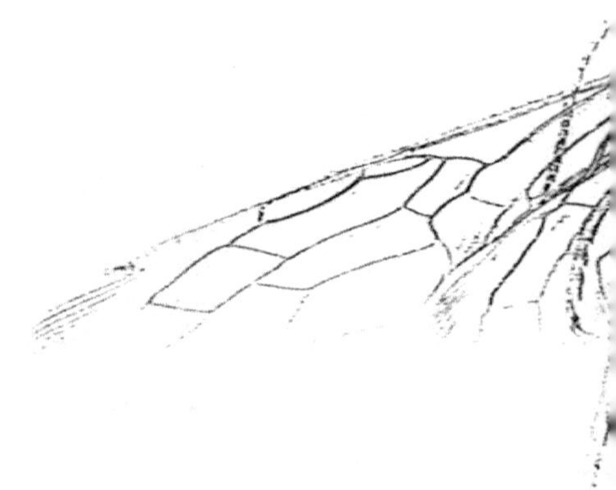

iowa poems

FIGURE № 1: WING

Right away the doctor and his pretty
Little nurse insisted that it mattered
What's beneath the face of a clown.
You said it's all just surface
The tears painted black upon his cheek
And that fantastic red mouth
Which is always downturned.

FIGURE № 2: BUTTERFLY or MOTH

Citing passage and verse
You proved how he spoke
Through Revelations, which was
Really nothing new, a divine purpose.
You explained that spectacles are
The most persuasive way to salvation
And why you wanted
To announce the solution at the Rose Bowl

But you had to be careful
On the next page was the devil,
His spiny nose in the most harmless of place
Made you preoccupied
With more difficult things
Your hands are starting to twitch.

FIGURE № 3: A BOW TIE

They exchange knowing looks,
A silent decision.
When you told them that
Around his invisible neck
Was a black lamb in repose.
Explaining how he rewarded your meek-
    ness,
Second of three and the slowest one,
How he helped you remember

High school freshmen laughing
At their overgrown classmate
While they still dreamed of puberty.
Not quite eighteen and according
To Rorschach, an F minus.
It was the usual and unimportant
That day you went into the hospital.

FIGURE № 5: BUTTERFLY FEELERS or RABBIT EARS

The doctor became interested again
When you said it looked like something
Out of a nightmare, mother locking
You in a room, suspicious of the trouble
Which children usually make.
She was quite and serious and said
She did it all for love
And you believed her, knowing
Only that which your hands could touch.

Hidden under the bed at night
You told them you could feel,
Yes, feel right through the mattress
The horns in velvet of a devil.

FIGURE № 6: FLOWER PETALS or THE TIPS OF WINGS

A bell-shaped curve
Determines the true form of health.
Out along its trailing edge, your father
Indecisive, could never cope.
He was called a poor provider
But he didn't want to be
Either poor or a provider.

Yet you couldn't explain
Why it made you angry
To mention they were his
Those stinking feet of adultery.

FIGURE № 8: TWO DETAILS –
SMALL HUMAN FIGURES

Then the succession of pictures began
To make sense, the engorged heads of arrows
Pointing towards heaven was a warning
About how this trial would end,
And you didn't recognize
Until much later, there is no more room
For prophets. Still you have tried to convince
Them of your power over a little girl

Who waited outside for a pronouncement,
A story already written
About freedom's mistakes

FIGURE № 8b: TWO DETAILS – ROCKS or FLOWER PETALS or COWS' HEADS

They had to prove your insanity
Their justification. It is still
Almost treasonous as visions are
Reserved for only prophets and madmen.
"It is a face, no, two faces of women
Looking up at the sun."

But that was somehow against the rules
Recognized on earth in three people,
The wife, the princess and our judge, the doctor.

FIGURE № 9: THE FACE
OF A WOMAN

With that long curly hair,
Those smooth and beardless cheeks,
It had to be
David Lloyd George or Josiah Royce.
They were special because they never laughed,
For a few odd jobs you could earn
Bits of hard candy to suck
Between your teeth.

It took all this time to learn
That men can be better mothers
Than the ones we find in nature

FIGURE № 10: TWO DETAILS – LION or DOG REARING ON ITS HAUNCHES

No matter what arguments are used
It is constantly forgotten
That your special character of beauty
Is the stuff of imagination
Which needs no security and that for all
The precise formulations, nature
Succeeds for the most part

Only because there is something
Vaguely positive in reproduction
All those cells dividing, sometimes
Creating, sometimes not.
The last picture told it all,
A man bowing his head
To the collapsed figure of a woman.

Michael Shay was born in Ludwigshafen am Rhein, Germany, & grew up in Chicago. At the University of Iowa he studied with Louise Glück, was chosen to attend the summer session of the Iowa Graduate Poetry Workshop, & studied with Marvin Bell. He also holds a Master Of Creative Arts In Interdisciplinary & Experimental Art. Michael's work has appeared in literary journals including *The South Carolina Review*, *Nimrod* and *Rhino*. He was contributing ed. to *Broken Word* (The Alberta St. Anthology) Vols. I & II. A commercial photographer, Michael also writes, delights in his grandchild, practices martial arts, brews his own beer, & lives in Portland, Oregon.

— ○ ◯ ○ —

Also available from Reprobate Books & GobQ

El Gato Eficaz /Deathcats, Luisa Valenzuela (winner, 2019 Carlos Fuentez Prize), *tr., Jonathan Tittler* (*en-face* bilingual ed.), ISBN: 978-1-93566-234-1, $12

↖↗

America the Beautiful & other indictments (a meaningful life 2.0, txt-only, ed.), Christoph Keller ISBN 978-1-64764-361-4, $12.00

↖↗

Appendix A: Sound Seekers: File Under Jazz, Christoph Keller ISBN 978-1-64764-391-1, $10.00

↖↗

The Art of Waking Up: 62 Poems & a Song of Despair (Rev., 2nd ed., incl. recent poems), Brenda Taulbee, ISBN: 978-1-68454-469-1 \ | / $15

↖↗

The Jesus He Deserved, & Other Thoughts on War & on Returning, Sean Davis, Matthew Robinson, & Jacob Meeks, ISBN: 978-1-64204-581-9 $17

↖↗

A White Concrete Day: Poems, 1978 – 2013, Douglas Spangle, ISBN: 978-1-62847-660-6, $15

↖↗

the crucifXes & other friday poems, M. F. McAuliffe, ISBN: 978-1-68419-5338-1, $15

↖↗

Breakfast: 43 Poems, Coleman Stevenson, ISBN 978-194384465-4 , $15

↖↗

International trade distrib. through Ingram Spark

Ebook eds. forthcoming through Ingram Spark/Lightning Source, Kobo, Nook/Barnes&Noble.

↖↗ ↖↗ ↖↗ ↖↗ ↖↗ ↖↗ ↖↗ ↖↗ ↖↗ ↖↗ ↖↗ ↖↗

SHOEGAZE BOOKS, distrib through GobQ/Reprobate Books & Ingram Spark

Seattle, M.F. McAuliffe, ISBN 978-1-94424441-5, $12 (Also available in a Digital Ed., pub. Sept., 2015, ISBN 978-1-943843-27-5)

↖↗ ↖↗ ↖↗ ↖↗ ↖↗ ↖↗ ↖↗ ↖↗ ↖↗ ↖↗ ↖↗ ↖↗

Seek ye special chappy & flip books, incl. Lithuanian, Croatian & Israeli en-face collections, graphic novels & anthologies, & other textual & visual marvels fr. late 2020 & beyond

— ○ ◯ ○ —

Gobshite Quarterly no. 35/36, Winter/Spring 2020, $12.

(all back issues avail. online X; issues #19/20 & after distrib. internationally through Ingram Spark/Lightning Source POD, & can be ordered fr. independent boostores)

— ○ ◯ ○ —

www.ingramcontent.com/pod-product-compliance
Lightning Source LLC
Chambersburg PA
CBHW051811050726
47598CB00006B/2508